STEPHEN,

Estéban (or Estevanico—Stephen) for five years after Narváez's disastrous withdrawal from Florida travelled westward across the North American continent. With famed Cabeza de Vaca and two others, Stephen made an adventurous crossing of New Mexico and Arizona, meeting great hardships along the way. Their reports to Viceroy Mendoza when they finally found their way to Mexico City inspired the great Cíbola expedition of Vásquez de Coronado in 1540. The Viceroy sent Stephen back northward and he became guide for the first exploration of our Southwest, which in time would be covered with huge ranchos worked by *vaqueros*-the cowboys. Stephen was the first there of all those who came from the Old World. He led the way.

Today between the Mississippi and the Pacific there are many ranches and cowboys. But early in the last century nearly all this land was unexplored wilderness, inhabited by the great warlike nations. Mostly only daring fur trappers visited there, and the most daring was Jim Beckwourth of the Rocky Mountain Fur Co. In his immortal *Autobiography* he tells of myriad adventures. But besides giving us his great book and exploring lands where cowboys followed, he discovered a mountain pass of immense value.

"The fame of Jim **BECKWOURTH** was celebrated by all tongues." *We struck across...to the waters of the Truchy, which latter flowed in an easterly direction, telling us we were on the eastern slope of the mountain range. This, I at once saw, would afford the best wagon-road...approaching from the eastward...A northern route had been discovered.*

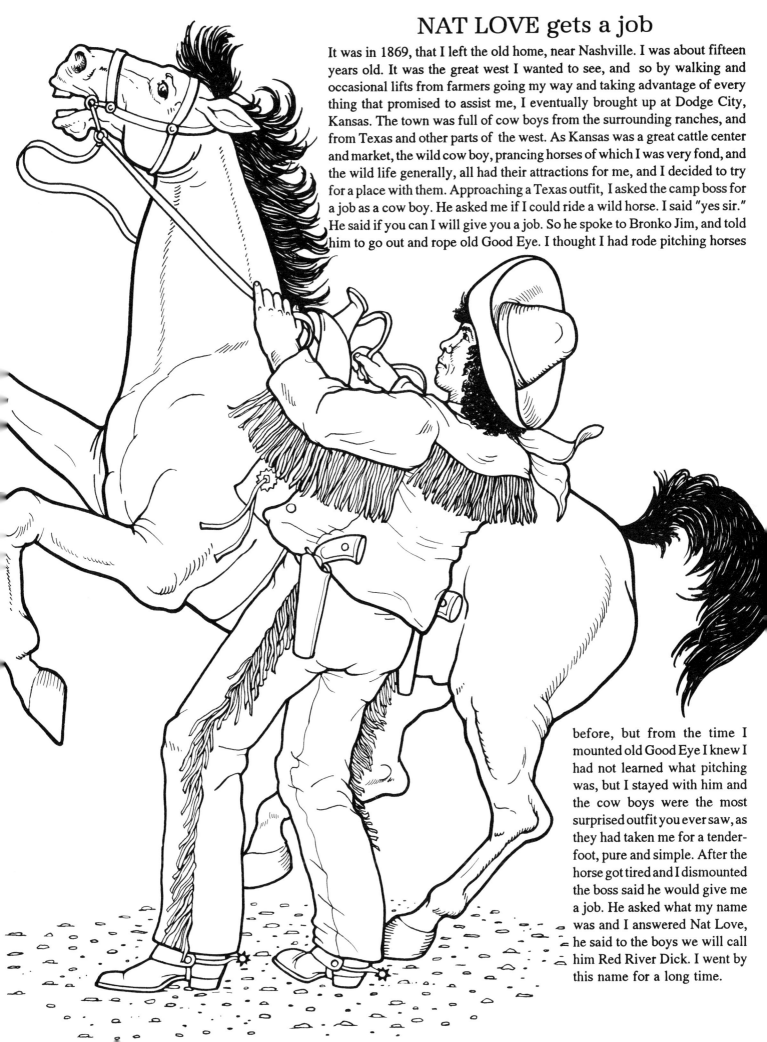

NAT LOVE gets a job

It was in 1869, that I left the old home, near Nashville. I was about fifteen years old. It was the great west I wanted to see, and so by walking and occasional lifts from farmers going my way and taking advantage of every thing that promised to assist me, I eventually brought up at Dodge City, Kansas. The town was full of cow boys from the surrounding ranches, and from Texas and other parts of the west. As Kansas was a great cattle center and market, the wild cow boy, prancing horses of which I was very fond, and the wild life generally, all had their attractions for me, and I decided to try for a place with them. Approaching a Texas outfit, I asked the camp boss for a job as a cow boy. He asked me if I could ride a wild horse. I said "yes sir." He said if you can I will give you a job. So he spoke to Bronko Jim, and told him to go out and rope old Good Eye. I thought I had rode pitching horses

before, but from the time I mounted old Good Eye I knew I had not learned what pitching was, but I stayed with him and the cow boys were the most surprised outfit you ever saw, as they had taken me for a tenderfoot, pure and simple. After the horse got tired and I dismounted the boss said he would give me a job. He asked what my name was and I answered Nat Love, he said to the boys we will call him Red River Dick. I went by this name for a long time.

TOM BASS
The World's Greatest Horseman
1859-1939

Before automobiles, horses were everything. And the beautiful horses trained by gentlemanly Tom Bass from Mexico, Missouri, are part of American equine history. Probably nobody ever understood horses as well as Tom Bass. He invented a new bit, to make training horses more comfortable. Bits had been cruel things before. His most important contribution was teaching his horses complicated routines. Tom had begun training horses when he was seven years old. When he was in his teens he was called "the best judge of horses" known. He would take a wild horse, which others had failed to train, and train it beautifully. People longed to own championship horses, and Tom's were champions. His world-famous horses were owned by presidents, and he was a personal friend of Presidents Cleveland, Mc Kinley, Roosevelt and Taft, who visited him in Missouri. Buffalo Bill Cody bought Tom's gorgeous Columbus. Tom, the first Black to show in St. Louis, became immensely popular there, where he showed Columbus. Tom's black stallion, Rex Mc Donald, became America's greatest saddle horse, "king of the breed." His Miss Rex, a beautiful silver mare, also won many championships. Tom once took a badly injured yearling and turned her into America's greatest show mare, Belle Beach. Her dancing was "eyepoppin'."

THE BUFFALO SOLDIERS

The Black troopers of the Ninth and Tenth U. S. Cavalry fought the fights which opened the west for ranching and cowboys. Their duties were patrolling the frontier with endless marching over deserts and mountains, protecting the mail and stage route, and establishing law and order. Their military service was "as onerous and as barren of opportunities for achieving renown as ever fell to soldiers in any land. They cannot attack the enemy, whip him, and be done with it. They seldom have the pleasure of a battle, but they may at any time suffer an attack. They have to do a sort of police service, which may on a sudden become warfare over a large area...The troopers...are men who are never safe from death by an Apache surprise. Their camp may any night be their burial place. But they can never be surprised out of a heroic mood."—*Harper's Weekly*, August 21, 1886. "...anyhow, the Tenth Cavalry never had a 'soft detail' since it was organized (1866), and it is full of old soldiers who know what it is all about, this soldiering...And it rains, rains, rains, as mile after mile the little column goes

After Remington, 1888

bobity-bobity-bob up and down over the hills. But I like it...The soldiers like it too." "They may be tired and they may be hungry, but they do not see fit to augment their misery by finding fault with everybody and everything. In this particular they are charming men with whom to serve." — Frederic Remington, "Vagabonding with the Tenth Horse," and "A Scout with the Buffalo Soldiers," *Century Magazine*, 1897 and 1889. "I cannot speak too highly of the conduct of the officers and men under my command, always cheerful and ready, braving the severest hardships with short rations and no water without a murmur." — Major Morrow, June 1, 1870, regarding the Ninth Cavalry who had just "marched about 1,000 miles over two hundred of which was through country never explored by troops."

The Black "Buffalo Soldiers" found themselves in many, many Western fights. And from these, against the bravest and fiercest of adversaries, they invariably came off the field true heroes; they were among the very best soldiers in all of our history. "They were determined that no soldiering should be carried on in which their valor was not proved," said Mrs. Custer. They were painted and drawn by the great American artist Frederic Remington. He had the utmost esteem for the Black troopers, and he made them immortal.

A magnificent monument commemorating these great Black soldiers has just been dedicated at Fort Leavenworth, Kansas, by General Colin Powell, Chairman, Joint Chiefs of Staff.

Arms of the Tenth Regiment
U. S. Cavalry, c. 1920.

The Tenth U. S. Cavalry Regiment in Arizona, 1888

Dark blue shirts, light blue trousers with yellow stripe.

"In the early days of April last, the hostiles, then in Sonora, Mexico, began their depredations, and on the 27th of that month invaded the territory of Arizona. They at once met active opposition; Captain T. C. Lebo, Tenth Cavalry, true to his reputation as a gallant and successful cavalry leader, moving first against them. He followed the hostiles rapidly for over two hundred miles, and finally, on May 3rd, forced them to an encounter. During this spirited engagement the officers and men evinced great bravery, contending against an enemy on ground of their own choosing, among rugged cliffs almost inaccessible. During the engagement, Corporal Scott, a brave soldier, lay disabled with a serious wound, exposed to the enemy's fire, and Lieutenant P. H. Clark, Tenth Cavalry, rushed to his assistance, carrying him to a place of safety. Such acts of heroism are worthy of great praise."—Capt. Thomspon, Oct. 7, 1886.

"(They) have cheerfully endured many hardships and privations, and in the midst of great dangers steadfastly maintained a most gallant and zealous devotion to duty, and they may well be proud of the record made, and rest assured that the hard work undergone in the accomplishment of such important and valuable service to their country, is well understood and appreciated, and that it cannot fail, sooner or later, to meet with due recognition and reward.

"That the high standard of excellence gained by the regiment for discipline and efficiency in the past will be fully sustained in the future; that the most signal success will ever attend the officers and soldiers of the Tenth Cavalry in all their noble efforts and undertakings, official or otherwise, is the heartfelt wish of their old commander."—Col. Grierson, Dec. 1, 1888.

Both after Frederic Remington, 1888

TENTH CAVALRY

A Buffalo Soldier of the tough
Twenty-fifth U. S. Infantry Regiment

The Black Cowboy in Fiction:
"But what of THE EBONY STAR? a prodigious feat he performed..."
as he bent over and saved...

ARIZONA

The Twenty-fourth & Twenty-fifth infantry were established in 1869, and marched across the deserts and mountains of the West, and where adversaries believed that no soldier could ever go. "I never witnessed better courage or better fighting..."—Medal of Honor file of Sgt. Benj. Brown, 1889. "...there are no better troops in the service...They are model soldiers...The Twenty-fifth Infantry. It is a splendid regiment and worthy of unstinted praise." *Anaconda Standard*, Aug. 6, 1924

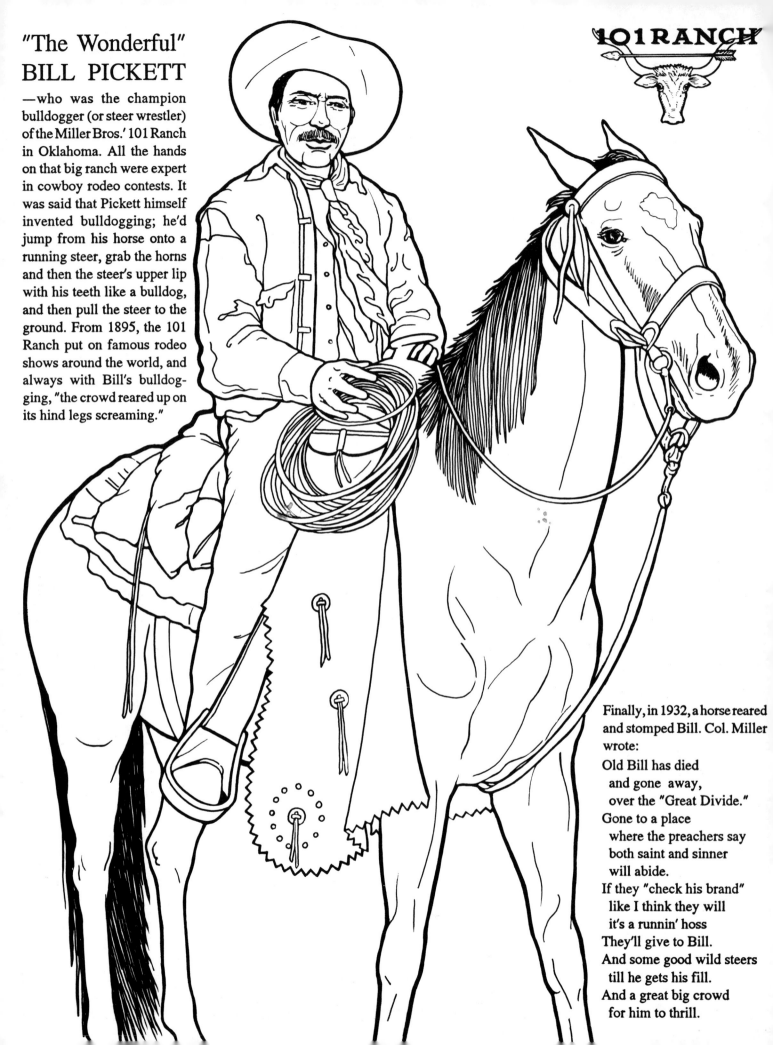

"The Wonderful" BILL PICKETT

—who was the champion bulldogger (or steer wrestler) of the Miller Bros.' 101 Ranch in Oklahoma. All the hands on that big ranch were expert in cowboy rodeo contests. It was said that Pickett himself invented bulldogging; he'd jump from his horse onto a running steer, grab the horns and then the steer's upper lip with his teeth like a bulldog, and then pull the steer to the ground. From 1895, the 101 Ranch put on famous rodeo shows around the world, and always with Bill's bulldogging, "the crowd reared up on its hind legs screaming."

101 RANCH

Finally, in 1932, a horse reared and stomped Bill. Col. Miller wrote:

Old Bill has died
 and gone away,
 over the "Great Divide."
Gone to a place
 where the preachers say
 both saint and sinner
 will abide.
If they "check his brand"
 like I think they will
 it's a runnin' hoss
They'll give to Bill.
And some good wild steers
 till he gets his fill.
And a great big crowd
 for him to thrill.

NED HUDDLESTON, also known as the Black Fox and as Isom Dart, was "one of the best cowboys ever to mount a horse in the high mesa country." Born a slave, when free after the Civil War Ned went to Texas and then on to Brown's Hole, Colorado; he dealt in pre-owned horses, not bothering with making payment for them. He also caught and broke wild horses, and was said to be the best bronco rider ever. In order to feed a neighbor's large family, Ned did a bit of rustling. A deputy sheriff was sent to arrest Ned; a wheel fell off the deputy's buckboard and the lawman was injured. Ned took care of the hurt man; he took him to the hospital and himself to the jail. When Ned went to trial, the recovered deputy told the jury about what Ned had done. Of course the jury let him go. But Ned again rustled cattle, and Tom Horn, a ranch detective, shot him. Ned was buried on Cold Spring Mountain early in 1900; "for all-around skill as a cowman," said a neighbor about Ned, he "was unexcelled and I never saw his peer.".

MYRTIS DIGHTMAN

"Play it cool and take your time."

"I just like to rodeo," said Myrtis, the oldest competing bull rider. He spent years on the circuit of the Rodeo Cowboys Association, sometimes riding three bulls a day, holding on with one hand to a rope for eight seconds around one mean bull after another. Rider and bull are both scored—the bull by his toughness to ride and the rider by his skill. Myrtis won his way to the finals seven times, based upon his success at winning prize money. Bull riding is one of six championship events; others are steer wrestling, bronco riding, calf roping and cowgirl racing. It is a dangerous business. Lawrence Reed, a Black cowboy who started in rodeo when Myrtis began, was killed by a bull. Cowboy Reed left a wife and six children. "I never liked riding bulls," said Myrtis, "but I did love the challenge."

CHARLES SAMPSON, World Champion Bull Rider

—grew up in Watts, the eleventh of thirteen children; he was just five feet three inches tall. When he was a ten-year-old Cub Scout, he had taken a twenty-five-cent pony ride and he was hooked. Myrtis told Sampson to finish school; he'd help him if he did. Sampson graduated on crutches, for a bull had already crushed him. He then got a scholarship to college and joined the rodeo team. He then rode thirty or more mean bulls a month professionally, and one day was thrown from five bulls in three states. He was ready to quit; he had had his leg broken three times, broken arms, broken fingers, broken jaw, broken feet and more near-fatal wounds would follow. But his partner said that to win the World Championship, the only way was to keep going. And in 1982 he did indeed receive the trophy and buckle as Champion Bull Rider of the World. "I'm proud," said his friend Myrtis, "a black man has won." Sampson talked in the schools: "There is no goal that can't be reached with determination and positive thinking," he said.

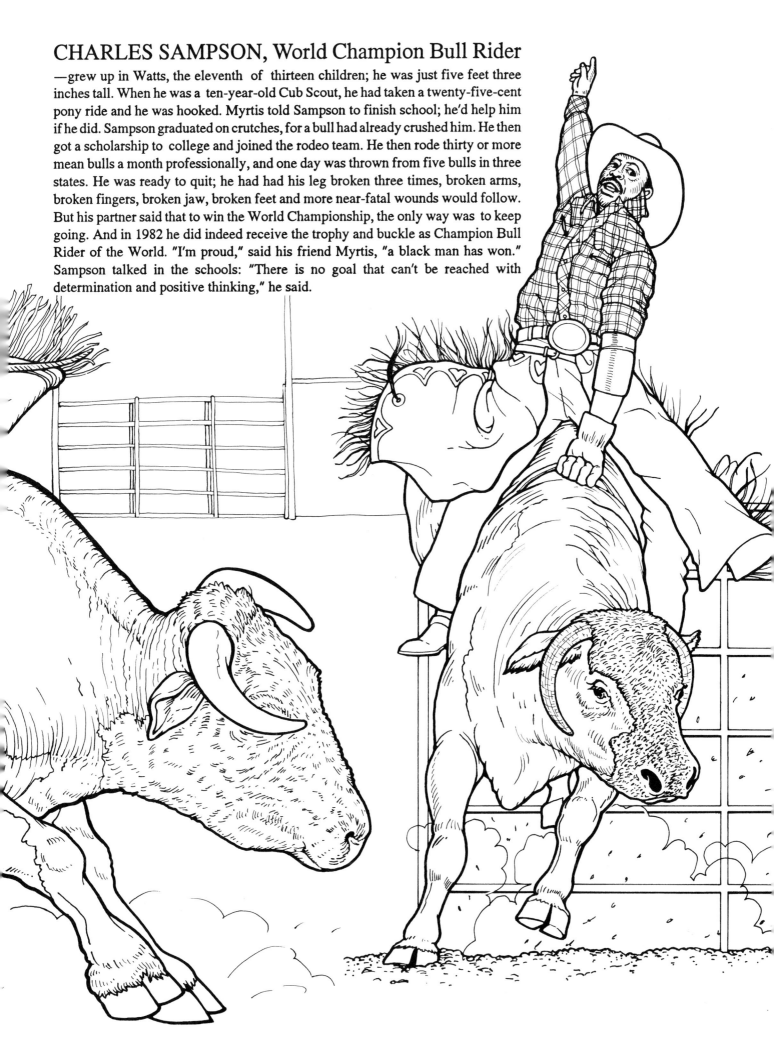

FRED WHITFIELD
The Calf Roper

Fred grew up in Cypress, Texas, near Houston, and began riding horses when he was five and roping when he was seven—roping chickens, the mail box and his mom. In his first rodeo at age nine, he successfully roped his calf and rode his steer and won in each event. The next round he missed the calf and the steer threw him. "I learned how quick the world of rodeo changes," he said. At fifteen he rode his first and last bulls; having kissed one right between the horns, Fred decided he liked calf roping better. Fred is big—six feet three inches, and is fairly recent on the professional circuit. He had watched some of the top ropers and said to himself, "I'm just as good as those guys," and sure enough—he was. He would win in Calgary, Kansas City and the "Daddy of 'em all," Cheyenne, and become PCRA Rookie of the Year in 1990. "Rodeo's the greatest thing. I love it, " says Fred. "The door's wide open; the only thing I've got to do is go through it."

LEON COFFEE,
Bull-fighting Rodeo Clown

Leon's from Austin, Texas, and he travels about 68,000 miles a year in his pickup truck as a top clown in the PCRA rodeo circuit. In school he had been an all-state line backer, and he's an athlete with lightning speed. For fourteen years he was a bull rider, and he knows how much bull riders depend on the clown to get them away from disaster. For when a bull rider is thrown or getting off, the clown leaps to take the animal's attention so the rider can escape unhurt. Leon truly tickles the fans with wonderful tricks and dances as he rescues the riders, who for their part give him heartfelt thanks. His is dangerous work. He tries to be on the bull's head the instant the cowboy starts off. "I slapped one old bull and he slapped me back," said Leon. The hospital resulted, but Leon is nimble and usually outruns the bulls. "God put me on Earth for two things—to help people out and to make people happy. I can do both as a clown," he says. "I just eat, sleep, breathe and live for rodeos," he adds in spite of his ribs having been crushed, his face remade and rewired, and lots of bones broken. "Why not go for the gusto?" he asks.

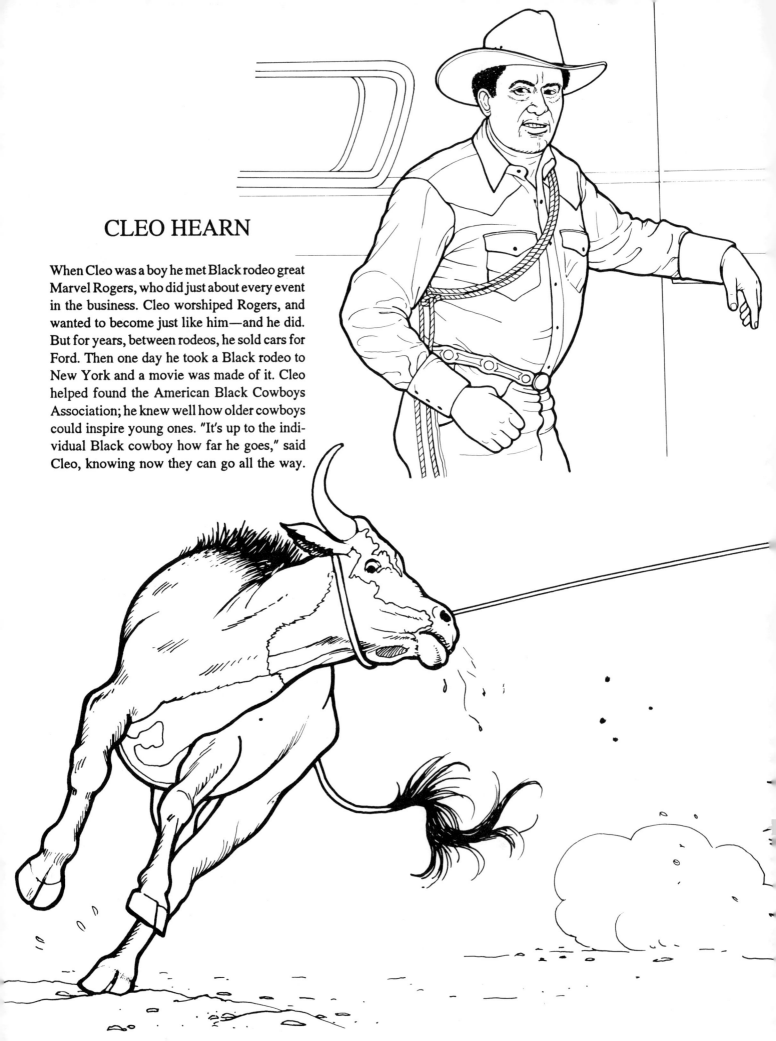

CLEO HEARN

When Cleo was a boy he met Black rodeo great Marvel Rogers, who did just about every event in the business. Cleo worshiped Rogers, and wanted to become just like him—and he did. But for years, between rodeos, he sold cars for Ford. Then one day he took a Black rodeo to New York and a movie was made of it. Cleo helped found the American Black Cowboys Association; he knew well how older cowboys could inspire young ones. "It's up to the individual Black cowboy how far he goes," said Cleo, knowing now they can go all the way.

JESSE JAMES
and his horse Spook

He's from a ranch near Porterville, California.
Jesse started rodeoing young, riding bulls and
then switching to calf roping and team compe-
tition. Now he has his own ranch of 2,000 acres
plus about 40,000 acres more of leased gov-
ernment grazing land. While doing his chores
he works out his horses and calves. With all his
ranch experience, Jesse won the calf-roping
event in the National Finals.

A Young Cowboy Today

Spud Venerable of Kansas City, Kansas, prepares to rope a calf.

Paul Stewart tells about the Black West, right.

Mr. Stewart founded the Black American West Museum in Denver, Colorado. Of course the West has a full and rich history of Black men, women and children, who were as much a part of it as anyone. In the California Gold Rush, for instance, Black miners were considered lucky—and many were very lucky. Others thought themselves fortunate to work along side them. And on the great cattle drives of the plains Black cowboys were very well represented and their abilities were ever lauded. When you go to Denver, you must visit the Black American West Museum; it's great.

DWAYNE HARGO,
World Champion Rodeo Clown,
the second Black cowboy to win a world title

Dwayne's from Placerville in the California gold country. As a boy, he worked in a stable in exchange for the use of a horse. When he was thirteen, he began working for a rodeo company. He fed the bulls and watered the horses and set up the stands. Dwayne graduated from high school, and then he took a course from one of the great bullfighter clowns. Soon he came to be known as a gutsy, very entertaining cowboy clown. He has won the World Championship as Wrangler (the cowboy pants maker) Bullfighter. In this event, points are given for how aggressive both bull and bullfighter (the clown) are, and how well the bullfighter controls the bull. Of course, the bull isn't hurt in this kind of bullfighting. But the bullfighter rodeo clown can't always say that for himself. The Sportswriters of America have voted this as the country's most dangerous sport.